COLLECT THIS!

A Cool Guide to Collecting for Kids

Written by Donna Guthrie and Christy Zatkin

Illustrated by Larry Ross

PSS!
PRICE STERN SLOAN

To Jason — DWG

My thanks to Howard for supporting me,
to Geoffery and Cynthia for encouraging me,
and to Donna for inviting me to write with her — CZ

Trademark note: All terms mentioned in the book that are known to be registered trademarks, trademarks, or service marks have been appropriately capitalized when we are aware of them. Price Stern Sloan cannot attest to the accuracy of this information. The use of a term in this book should not be regarded as affecting the validity of any registered trademark, trademark, or service mark.

Text copyright © 2001 by Donna Guthrie and Christy Zatkin. Illustrations copyright © 2001 by Larry Ross. All rights reserved. Published by Price Stern Sloan, a division of Penguin Putnam Books for Young Readers, New York. Printed in the United States of America. Published simultaneously in Canada. No part of this publication may be reproduced, stored in any retrieval system, or transmitted, in any form or by any means, electronic, mechanical, photocopying, recording, or otherwise, without the prior written permission of the publisher.

Library of Congress Cataloging-in-Publication Data is available.

ISBN 0-8431-7658-X   A B C D E F G H I J

PSS!® is a registered trademark of Penguin Putnam Inc.

Contents

Introduction 1

Chapter 1   Collecting Basics 3

Chapter 2   Building Your Collection .15

Chapter 3   Collecting from Stores 31

Chapter 4   Moving Outdoors 45

Chapter 5   Organizing It All 61

Chapter 6   Clubs, Conventions, and a Few Things More 79

introduction

People love to collect things.

Do you walk along the beach and pick up shells? Are your pockets filled with rocks or bubble gum wrappers? Do you save your books even though you've read them a hundred times? Do you keep toys from when you were a toddler? Are your shelves filled with hats, dolls, or mugs? Do you keep the fortunes from fortune cookies, or the caps from bottles? Are you amazed at the perfectly good things people throw away? Do people complain about your clutter?

If you answered yes to even a few of these questions, chances are you're a collector.

Maybe you already know you're a collector. If so, what condition is your collection in? Are the things that you like to collect collecting dust? Are they shoved under the bed or stuffed in the closet? Are they piled up or scattered about?

The right display can make all the difference in whether you've got a collection or just clutter. There's an old saying that "One man's trash is another man's treasure."

Maybe it's time to turn your "trash" into treasure. With a little bit of energy and a whole lot of fun, you can organize, categorize, and display those rocks, shells, and bubble gum wrappers.

Collecting can open up a whole new world! There are people out there who collect the things you love, as well as things you might consider strange or weird. Collectors have their own clubs, magazines, conventions, and websites. There are even ways to buy, auction, and trade your collection without leaving your house.

So let's get started! Ready, set, collect!

CHAPTER 1
Collecting Basics

What to Collect?
The Invisible Collection

Walk into your room and take a look around. Start with your window ledge. Are there rocks from a hike you took last summer or seashells from the beach? Take a peek under the bed. Are your old trains or the plastic toys from your favorite fast food restaurant scattered among the dust balls?

Open your closet door. Do you have three PEZ dispensers, four floaty pens, or six Matchbox cars in that box you couldn't throw away? If you're lucky enough to have a basement or an attic, grab a flashlight and go exploring. Is this where your mom stored your five-piece wooden puzzles or the picture books you loved? If you're really lucky, you might find her forgotten autograph book or your dad's old baseball cards.

You get the idea. **Begin with what you have.** You may already have an "invisible collection," or interesting stuff that could be expanded, developed, and grown into a real collection.

> **The Cool Collector says:** Find a friend who wants to collect, too.

Starting from Scratch

Okay, so you've explored your house and there's nothing that grabs your attention. Daydream for a minute. What fires up your imagination? What gets you excited? Do you love baseball or botany? Are you a ballet dancer or a Boy Scout? Do you dream of traveling to Bali or Baltimore, or do you prefer your own backyard? Collectors collect around their own interests. When you're not in school, what do you do? Sing soprano in the church choir? Toot a tuba? Raise longhaired guinea pigs? Or go skateboarding? Jump from your interest into a collection.

It also helps if you decide on something that you can actually find. (Moon rocks might not be a good idea!) Autographs, teddy bears, and baseball caps can be found worldwide. This makes them fun and easy to collect. Every time you attend a game, you can bring home a different baseball cap. You can ask your aunts and uncles for a cap from their city's team. They might even have an old hat from when the Los Angeles Dodgers were the Brooklyn Dodgers. That's a collectible! Letting friends and relatives know what you collect gives them ideas for presents, too. That's a great way to grow your collection.

Collecting Comment

The Greek word for a lover of something is *phil*. A lover, or collector, of books is a biblio*phile*, a lover of stamps is a *phil*-atelist, a lover of flowers is an anthro*phile*, and someone who loves cats is an ailuro*phile*.

Theme Collections

In a world of stuff to collect, themes give direction to your collections. Are your action figures from the same movie? If you loved the film, look for all the things that go with it like posters, lunch boxes, school supplies, clothing, magnets, and mugs. That's the beginning of a theme collection. Follow it.

A Cool Collection

The National Baseball Hall of Fame and Museum in Cooperstown, New York, is the ultimate theme collection. It collects everything that has to do with baseball. But Peter Clark, Curator of Collections, says the nuttiest baseball collection he's ever seen is the Boltman Baseball Team. Sometime in the 1960s a fan from Brooklyn collected screws, washers, nails, nuts, and bolts and assembled them into an entire baseball team mounted on a wooden baseball field. The Boltman Baseball Team is housed in the museum.

The Cool Collector says: You can declare a collection complete. Nobody says you have to go on forever. You may end one collection and start another.

Set Collections

Autographs, baseball caps, bears, and magnets are unending collections. Other things come in sets. What's nice about a set collection is the sense of accomplishment that comes when a set is complete. If you are a sports fan, collecting caps or autographs from hockey, baseball, basketball, soccer, football, and auto racing would be expensive and hard to manage. Set collecting directs you to one sport. One cap from each of the major league baseball teams is a set. Another set would be all the autographs from your favorite soccer team. Or, if you're stuck on magnets, one from each of the fifty states would be a set collection.

A Bright idea

Branch out. Find your roots. Create a family tree with photographs. How many generations of faces can you collect? Parents and grandparents shouldn't be a problem, but what about great-grandparents and long-lost uncles? This collection can make you the family **genealogist**, the person who finds the family ancestors. As you collect the photographs, record as much information as possible: name, relationship to you, birth date, and place of birth. For more information about how to design a family tree, check out the genealogy website recommended by the International Scout Project and The National Science Project, http://home.earthlink.net/~howardorjeff/instruct.htm. From there you can link back to the project homepage.

Almost-Free Collections

Stores have fun, prepackaged, mass-produced collectibles. But they aren't the only way to go. Even if you don't have much money, you can still be a collector. You can have an unusual, one-of-a-kind, cool collection that reflects only you. Some of the most interesting collections have been started for pennies. For instance, that decoder ring your grandmother found in her cereal box when she was a little girl is now rare.

What are you throwing away today that might be valuable tomorrow? Fast food giveaways and Cracker Jack and cereal box prizes are free with the food—just like that old decoder ring. Decals, bumper stickers, political party pins, and promotional pens and pencils are some of today's throw-aways that could be tomorrow's treasures.

A Cool Collection

Mr. Graham Barker, who lives in Perth, Australia, has created a one of a kind collection that may take the "wacky" award. Since 1984, he has been collecting his own navel fluff (lint) and putting it in a glass jar. Why does he do this? According to him, collecting navel fluff doesn't take much time or space, and costs nothing. He says many people collect unusual things, such as airsickness bags, false teeth, old parking meters, and sugar packets. Mr. Barker encourages everybody to create wacky collections when he quotes G. K. Chesterton, "There are no uninteresting things, there are only uninterested people."

A Personal Collection

Are you throwing away what could be a personal collection? Presidents have libraries and athletes have halls of fame. All of these places are filled with keepsakes from a person's life. You may never be famous, but your life is worth remembering. Artwork, school papers, report cards, photographs, and awards would be a personal collection and a record of your life.

Collecting Comment

Animals collect things, too. The pack rat or desert wood rat loves to collect small, bright, shiny objects and hide them in his nest. People believe that this robber rodent is an honest thief—when he takes something he leaves something else in its place. Because this collecting rat can carry only one thing at a time, the rodent sometimes puts down one prize to pick up another.

Nature Collections

Some collections are right outside your door. Mother Nature offers butterflies, wildflowers, leaves, minerals, and shells to the nature-loving collector. Many of today's natural history museums showcase collections that were gathered, pressed, and mounted by ordinary people. Nature collections offer a deeper way to look at the world by showing you what's under your feet and over your head.

Why Collect?
Collecting for Love or Money

Once you've decided to become a collector, and maybe even what to collect, the next thing to think about is: Are you collecting for love or money?

If you're collecting for money, you expect the value of your collection to increase, so you can sell all or part of it for more than you paid for it. If you're collecting for love, you know the collection's value is in how much you enjoy it. It's probably never going to be just love or money because there's always a hint of both going on in any collection.

Value doesn't come just from money. Something you love and enjoy has value, too. Remember the songs you listened to again and again when you were little? Those tapes or CDs might not bring much at a garage sale, but you love them. Maybe that music was lost or thrown away and is no longer sold in music stores. If you found it in a

secondhand shop, you might be willing to pay more than the original price to make it part of your collection, because of **sentimental value**. Sentimental value is your emotional response to an object and sometimes determines **cash value**, how much you'll pay. Suppose you'd been searching stores and on the Internet for a long time before you located your lost music. That would mean it's **rare**, hard to find. Rarity makes something valuable. And if you found that music in **mint condition**, never used or like brand-new, you'd probably be willing to pay even more. Condition affects the cash value, too.

But who decides the cash value? For museums and large private collections, an **appraiser** does. An appraiser is someone who is trained to know rarity, condition, and cash value. People hire an appraiser so they won't sell something too low or buy it for too much. Beginning collectors don't need appraisers. They can find out prices from reading price guides, talking to other collectors, and attending shows and conventions.

Collecting for Money

What's the chance of finding that one special edition collectible card that you can resell for a million dollars—or even fifty dollars? Small. Very, very small. Tiny. If you are collecting for money, don't expect your collection to become valuable overnight. That's not going to happen. Why? Remember, rarity is one of the things that make something valuable. Collectible cards, Beanie Babies, and this year's fad are easy to collect because they're everywhere. That's the opposite of rare. If you don't mind waiting fifty years, what you're collecting, like your complete set of Star Wars figures, may be rare and valuable. Of course, there's a chance that thousands of other kids are stashing away their unopened boxes of young Luke Skywalker and Princess Leia, too.

You like the idea of collecting for future value? Great! Keep it fun by collecting something that interests you. Does a book you love have collectible characters? Does your favorite sport have collectible cards?

Let's pretend the newest fad is something called "yobos." Here are some collecting tips on how to collect for future value.

- ☐ Think complete sets—all the yellow yobos from Yozo; or all the yobos from the year you were born or the year you start your collection.
- ☐ Record the when and where of how each yobo came into your collection.
- ☐ Keep your yobo in its original, unopened package or in a collection book made for this type of yobo.
- ☐ File your receipts. That way you know your collection's original value and where it was purchased.
- ☐ Store or display your yobos out of the sun, so nothing gets faded or bleached out. Keep everything clean. If your friends roll their eyes at having

to wash their hands before admiring your latest yobo, too bad. You're a collector.

📋 Create a club or find a website for yobos so you can meet other yobo collectors.

Collecting for Love

Collecting for love means your collection may have value someday, but that's not your main goal. When you collect for love, you don't decide what to collect based on its cash value. Your collectible is valuable to *you*, and that's what counts. You may just think something is cool, or maybe it's been in your family for ages.

People who collect for love may not be as particular about the condition of their collection as people who collect for money. Let's say you're crazy about kazoos (toy whistles) and that's the reason you collect them. That's reason enough! If you have no plans to resell your kazoo collection, and you love to play your kazoos, go for it! You might want to start a club or find a website dedicated to kazoos so you can share your collection and encourage other lonely kazoo fans.

Other people who collect for love may be very concerned about the condition of their collection and keep their kazoos in the original boxes, and follow all the tips for future value. Either in or out of the box, where they came from and how much you paid for them applies to all collections. Who knows? Maybe one day your well-loved

kazoos will end up in a music museum. More likely, you'll enjoy showing them to your grandkids.

The World of Collecting

The world of collecting is deep and wide. Once you start exploring, you'll be amazed by the amount of things people collect, and the number of friendly people who are collectors. You'll discover clubs, conventions, shows, and auctions you can attend, and newsletters, magazines, and books devoted to almost every type of collectible. Many collectors end up with more than one collection. That may happen to you, too. Maybe you want a personal collection, a travel collection, and a sports collection. But watch out. Having too many collections is like channel surfing. You see a lot of action but you may miss the story.

True collectors are excited by the history and mystery of the objects they love. Like a good detective, they want

the story. If it's new, where did it come from? How did they get it? How does it add to their collection? If it's old, where did it come from? Who owned it? When was it made? How was it used? By uncovering and recording the details, collectors make their collections more valuable to themselves and maybe, eventually, to the world.

Collecting is not about how fast you can fill up shelves and boxes with the same kind of thing. It's about enjoying the experience of collecting, categorizing, preserving, and exhibiting the things you love.

CHAPTER 2
Building Your Collection

If you've looked around and, other than shoes and a few pairs of socks, you don't have two of anything, you're starting from scratch. There are lots of collecting possibilities right at home. Whether you are expanding or beginning a collection, a good way to begin building it is to think theme or think set.

Think Theme

Do your teddy bears have something in common? Are they all big bears, little bears, dressed bears, or bare bears? Grandma would love to know that you want a big black bear for your birthday. If your dad is traveling to Japan, put in a request for a bear dressed in a kimono. It's easier to expand a collection when other people know you're a collector and what you're looking for.

If you're starting from scratch, follow your interests to a theme. Do you love to skateboard? Consider a collection of skateboard decals, skateboard key rings, and skateboard posters.

Other types of theme collecting can be based on

television shows, movies, magazines, comic books, or whatever appeals to you. You can even invent your own theme.

> ### A Cool Collection
> The first bear in the Teddy Bear Museum in Naples, Florida, was a gift from a grandson to his grandmother. From this first bear, Frances Pew Hayes became an **arctophile** (a lover of teddy bears). She collected teddy bears on her travels and received them as gifts. When the bears and the people who wanted to see them reached overwhelming numbers, she started a museum. Each year around 45,000 people come to visit her growing collection of more than 3,000 bears.

A Personal Theme

You become the theme if you start a personal collection. Ask your mom or dad if they have a drawer filled with your papers and pictures. Take your art off the refrigerator and your bedroom walls. You'll have to be selective (until you have your own library or hall of fame!). Think in terms of a few special items from each year of your life. Create a portfolio starting with first grade or the earliest work you can find. Once you begin this collection, you can continue it from year to year.

What was the world like the year you were born? That's another idea for a personal collection. Start collecting things from that year, such as newspapers, magazines, books, posters, and calendars. Or begin a collection around your name. Collect miniature license plates,

pencils, pens, magnets, bookmarks, and mugs with your name on them.

An Animal Theme

Animals are a fun theme because they can be as unusual as aardvarks and armadillos, or as common as dogs and cats. You can find a theme within a theme like farm animals, zoo animals, or jungle animals. They don't have to be stuffed and cuddly. Any object is okay as long as it's your animal, and you like it.

Collecting Comment

In 1902, President Teddy Roosevelt and some of his friends went on a hunting trip in Mississippi. The only animal they found was a scared young bear. The president refused to shoot it. Cartoonist Clifford Berryman drew a cartoon of the president and the bear. Based on the cartoon, a toy maker created the first teddy bear and named it in the president's honor.

A Travel Theme

Theme collecting can give direction to your travel. Instead of wandering aimlessly around souvenir shops, you could be looking specifically for a cap from the Florida Marlins or a bear in a bikini. Travel can be a theme all by itself. Think about collecting a postcard, a spoon, a pin, a thimble, a miniature mug, a pencil, or a key chain from every new place you visit. Badges, decals, T-shirts, bumper stickers, pens, paperweights, letter openers—the list of travel collectibles is almost endless. To narrow things down you may want to try to focus on one or two—like pins or spoons.

Collectible Pins

Even before you climb in the car you can start a travel pin collection for free. Write to the KidsZone at 5758 Quarantine Court, Kearns, UT 84118. Tell them a little about yourself and what kind of pins you would like to collect. Make sure you include your return address in the letter. You can check out their website at www.pinfever.com/kidszone.html.

Souvenir Spoons

Stir up a taste for collecting with souvenir spoons. People have been collecting them since the late 1800s. Traveling is a good time to add to your spoon collection because hotels, restaurants, and resorts sell collectible spoons in their gift shops. For more information on how to get started in spoon collecting, check out the American Souvenir Spoons page at www.souvenirspoons.com or the Souvenir Spoon Museum at http://www.geocities.com/RodeoDrive/6232. Ask your relatives if they have one or two old souvenir spoons they'd like to donate.

A Matchless Collection

Matchbook covers are miniature billboards. This popular form of advertising can be the start of your collection. Don't use them, collect them. Keep them as you travel to document a trip, or collect around a theme such as banks, hotels, motels, cafes, and restaurants. There are more than 600 categories of match covers, and serious collectors search for them through clubs and over the Web. If you are interested in this free collectible, a good website is www.matchcovers.com.

Free and Almost-Free Theme Collections

Business cards and matchbooks are free. PEZ dispensers, the toys in kids' meals, and Cracker Jack and cereal box prizes all come with the food. Other ideas you can consider as a cash-conscious collector are stickers, pens, pencils, airsickness bags (unused), postal souvenir cards, decals, Band-Aids (unused), beads, buttons, theater programs, movie ticket stubs, used books, autographs, and canceled stamps.

A Cool Collection

For a cash-conscious collection, start with stickers. The big sticker debate is to stick or not to stick. Since they are so cheap, you could buy doubles. Paste one and preserve one. The ones you don't stick should be saved in acid free page protectors where they can be shown off for years to come. Places to stare at stickers are card, gift, and toy stores and on line at www.stickerplanet.com, or call Sticker Planet for its catalog at 1-800-557-8678.

Autographs

It's fun to have famous people sign your autograph book. But how do you meet them? You might get lucky and run into a celebrity at the airport. You could go to a game or a concert, fight your way through the crowd, and ask for it. But there's an easier and faster way to grow your autograph collection. Write a personal letter and make it simple for the person to reply. Enclose a stamped postcard for the celebrity to sign and send back.

Track down their addresses through their group, organization, or website. There's even a book titled *The Kid's Address Book: Over 3,000 Addresses of Celebrities, Athletes, Entertainers, and More*, by Michael Levine. Fan clubs are another way to get autographs and photos, but you may have to pay a membership fee. Lists of celebrities' addresses are also available for a cost. For more details on **philography** (autograph collecting), check http://kidscollecting.about.com and go to the link on autographs. This website has information about autographs and all sorts of other collections.

Once you track down the address, you're ready to write. There's a lot going on in a celebrity's life so it might take months for them to reply. Be patient; they're doing you a favor. It's a good idea to keep a copy of all your requests in a notebook so you know who you wrote to and when. Note the date they reply in your collecting notebook.

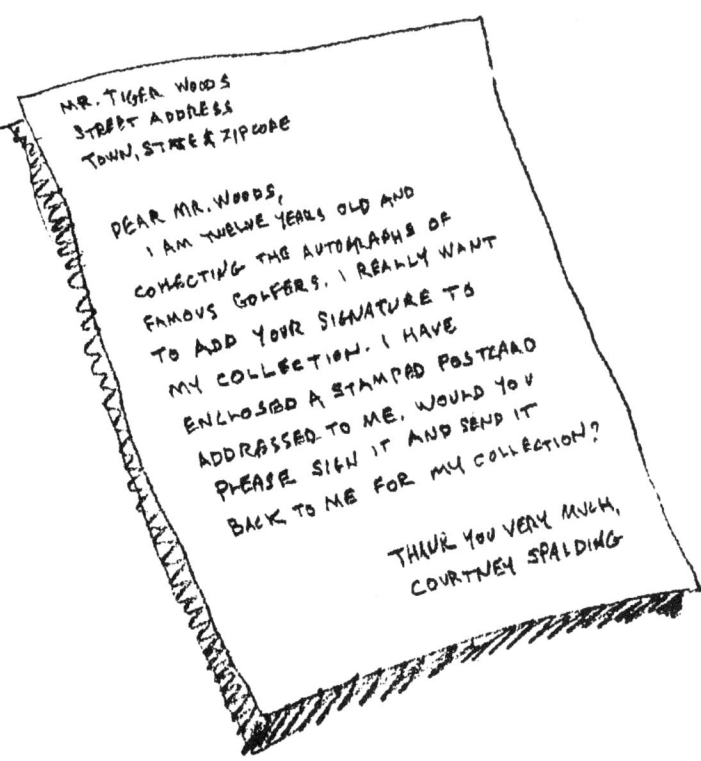

The Cool Collector says: There's a chance you could get an autographed picture and other cool stuff if you send a large envelope. With your letter, enclose a 9 by 12 inch envelope addressed to you and an index card for the autograph. Don't forget a bigger envelope needs more postage.

Stamps

To "stamp" out all costs, start a collection of canceled stamps from letters that come in the mail. Many **philatelists** (stamp collectors) collect only used stamps.

Think of all the stamps being delivered to your friends, neighbors, relatives, and teachers. Instead of throwing them in the trash, they could recycle them to you. Tell

them that you don't need the whole envelope, just the corner with the stamp.

If you find really old letters, you do want to keep the whole envelope because the postal markings can make the stamp even more valuable. Try finding longtime stamp collectors. They may have stamps they'd be willing to give you to help start your collection. They can also show you how a stamp hinge is used to attach the stamp to an album page without damaging the stamp.

Stamp collecting is a world of its own. To learn a staggering amount of stuff about stamps, send a business-size, self-addressed stamped envelope (SASE) to Junior Philatelists of America (JPA), P.O. Box 2625, Albany, OR 97321, or access the website at www.JPAstamps.org.

Do you need a direction for your stamp collection? You can be a **topical** stamp collector and focus on flowers,

birds, animals, famous people, presidents, space, sports, boats, or railroad trains. Postcard stamps are even a category for collecting.

A Bright idea

Commemorative stamps are issued to honor famous people, events, and places, and cost the same price as regular stamps. Ask people who write to you to use a different, commemorative stamp each time.

A Cool Collector

Franklin D. Roosevelt, the thirty-second president of the United States, collected stamps. His favorites were stamps from Hong Kong and the Americas. He started at age nine and continued his whole life. As president, he did have a slight advantage. He'd ask the assistant secretary of state to send him interesting foreign stamps. His collection grew to around 20,000 stamps. After his death, it was auctioned off for $230,000.

Postcards

If you don't want to stick with stamps, go for the bigger picture postcards. Along with stamps and coins, postcards are one of the top things people collect. Postcards have been around since 1893. Many postcard collectors focus on a topic or theme such as holidays, art, landscapes, animals, or silly photos. Let people know you're interested in **deltiology** (postcard collecting) and ask them to send you postcards when they travel.

You might want to join the International Postcard

Exchange, an organization dedicated to peace throughout the world by the exchange of postcards. There are more than 1,000 members in sixty-two countries. A one-time membership is $20 and comes with a club roster of postcard pen pals. Write to: Ms. Jennifer Batt, Executive Director, International Postcard Exchange (IPE), 7960 N.W. 50th Street #108, Lauderhill, FL 33351.

Collecting Comment

The Bureau of Engraving and Printing and the U.S. Postal Service create postal Souvenir Cards. They are issued for special stamp and coin shows and usually have pictures of old U.S. stamps or money. Prices range from one dollar to lots of dollars. You can find them at a local coin or stamp shop or on the Web at www.minnstamp.com/scard.htm or http://shop.usps.com.

Set Collecting

Theme collections can go on for a lifetime. You might prefer a collection with a beginning and an end. That's a set. Some sets you invent yourself. Other sets are created for you.

Let's say Freddie Patterson's Fast-Food Fish Factory brings out a set of six plastic fish every six months. You have four from the current set. It's time to catch the other two.

Do your friends or family eat at Freddie's? Will they collect for you or trade with you? Could your grandpa check out the Freddie's in his hometown for the missing fish? Once you've got all six, you've got your set!

New sets are always being invented. The United States Mint is offering a set collection in "mint" condition. Because Congress passed The Fifty States Commemorative Coin Program Act of 1997, each year through 2008 five

coins from five different states will be issued. Each state designs its own coin and the quarters are released in the order in which the states signed the Constitution or joined the Union. For more information on the world of coin collecting, look up the American Numismatic Association in the library or at www.money.org. Another site is the www.coinmasters.org and go to the Juniors link.

Themes Can Become Sets

A theme collection with a goal can become a set collection. For instance, instead of collecting spoons from every place you go for the rest of your life, you could collect one spoon for every national monument or state capital. If you are collecting animals, a goal could be to collect one animal for each letter of the alphabet.

Inventing Your Own Set

You can also invent your own set. For instance, there are fifty states in the United States and each one has a governor. (You knew that, didn't you?) What if you set a goal to collect each governor's autograph? Here's an address for all the states and their e-mail links: http://www.50states.com. (Or look in the library for a list of state tourism offices.)

There are fifty-four national parks. You could create a set of trail maps, postcards, or brochures—one from each park. For park collecting, check out this website, http://www.nps.gov or write the National Park Service for a list of parks and their addresses at National Park Service, 1849 C Street, NW, Washington, D.C. 20007.

During basketball season, you could collect team photos for that year from all the national basketball teams. Most of the major league sports teams send out free fan packs. Access this website and go to Teams at http://sportsillustrated.cnn.com to find addresses for all sorts of sports teams. Or you can call your hometown team and ask for the addresses of teams in their league.

Sets of national parks trail maps, governors' signatures, and team fan packs can be yours for the cost of the stamps it takes to write away for them. Two books that have addresses for free and inexpensive collectibles are *Free Stuff for Kids: 2001 Edition*, by the Free Stuff Editors, and *The Official Freebies for Kids* by the editors of Freebies magazine.

A Cool Collection

Can anything good come from being sick? It did for Don Brown, who spent a lot of time in the hospital when he was a little boy. One time as he was leaving, the head nurse gave him a string of prayer beads called a rosary. He began collecting rosaries from around the world and later became a Catholic. His collection numbers more than 4,000 rosaries, each carefully catalogued on when he got it, where it came from, and what it is made of. Today the collection is part of The Columbia Gorge Interpretive Center in Stevenson, Washington. Check out their website at http://columbiagorge.org.

Themes and Sets from Holidays

Collect around your culture or favorite holiday. Christmas ornaments, Hanukkah dreidels, and miniature skeletons from The Day of the Dead offer collecting possibilities for both sets and themes. Make a set each year of

the Christmas cards that come with family photographs. Make a theme collection around a holiday. For Valentine's Day you could collect cupids and hearts and valentines.

Kwanzaa is a holiday that started in 1966 to celebrate African American heritage, family, and culture. It's new enough that people may still have some cards and decorations from its early years. By starting a Kwanzaa collection now, you can follow the growth of this holiday in America.

Chapter 3
Collecting from Stores

Have you ever seen or heard of Smurfs, My Little Pony, or Pogs? A few years ago, they were fads just like Beanie Babies, Magic Cards, and Pokémon. Today, they're hard to find in stores, but there are still collectors and clubs devoted to them.

Some toys become so popular that people get crazy. They camp in front of stores, travel out of state, and pay huge amounts of money just to buy them. Next year or next month, this fad will pass and there will be another new "in thing" that everybody wants. Does that mean that fads aren't important? In the big scheme of world events, they aren't. But a fad can be a lot of fun!

How does a fad become a collection? That happens when the "in thing" becomes the "cherished thing," something you love, keep, and catalog. Fads are fabulous for theme collectors. Strike while the fad is hot and remember that theme collecting includes more than just the toy or doll. It is anything that is printed, stamped, embossed, or in any way marked with the collectible character. When a fad is at its peak, stores will be filled with fad paraphernalia like books, videos, CDs, T-shirts, lunch boxes, school supplies, backpacks, greeting cards, paper products, key chains, mugs, and posters.

On the other hand, one of the best times to start or expand a fad collection is after the fad peaks and everybody but you is looking for something new. That's when you find your collectible character in bargain bins and on sale tables.

New Collections

Toy stores, hobby shops, and game stores offer a vast number of collecting possibilities. Even something that is mass-marketed can become a personal collection.

Pokémon

Pokémon, those cute little critters found in video games, trading cards, and cartoons, may now be in a few bargain bins. If you are still enthralled with the 150 original characters and love the new edition, if you've seen the movies, own the videos, and still play Pokémon on your Game Boy . . . you're hooked. Don't worry about being

"out" instead of "in." Just like Cabbage Patch Kids dolls from the 1980s are still loved and collected by the people who grew up with them, you can continue to love and collect Pokémon.

The Cool Collector says: If you aren't a Pokémon fan, there may be other toys that fit in this category for you. You don't have to give up the toys you treasure even when their time in the spotlight is over.

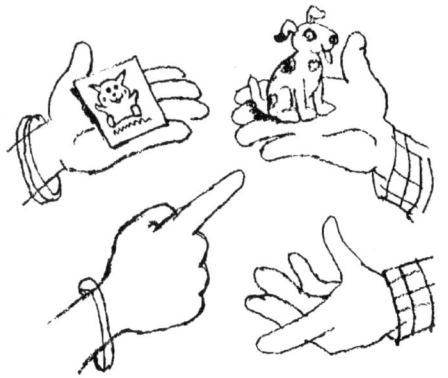

A Bright idea
When your friends tire of the latest fad and are ready to toss it, beg, bargain, or buy it—another source for expanding your collection.

Action Figures

Action figures are another type of toy that can easily become a collectible. You can start a theme collection and specialize in one kind of action figure, like G. I. Joe. Or you could have a set collection of all the action figures from the same story, comic book, or movie such as the X-Men.

Whether you play with your action figure or keep it in a box is up to you. In its original packaging it will have a higher future value. If the point of your collection is treasure, put it on display, out of the way. But if you're collecting for pleasure, treat your action figures gently (don't let your little brother pop off their heads or break their arms),

but go ahead and enjoy them. For more information about collecting action figures check out www.toymania.com and go to the action figure link.

> **Collecting Comment**
>
> G. I. Joe, the original action figure, marched into stores in the 1960s. He was twelve inches tall and carried a tommy gun or an M-1 rifle. In the 1980s, he shrank to three inches and updated his weaponry. For the twenty-first century he's back to his original size in the Classic Collection and carrying an MP-5 submachine gun and an M-203 rifle/grenade launcher. Each Classic G. I. Joe belongs to a different branch of the armed services. There is an Airborne Ranger, a U.S. Infantryman, a U.S. Marine, an Australian soldier, and a member of Britain's elite Special Air Service.

Collectible Card Games (CCGs)

Card games used to mean solitaire and Old Maid. Now you can deal a whole hand of collectible card games (CCGs) like Magic: The Gathering, Star Wars, Sailor

Moon, Dead Lands, Seventh Sea, Legend of the Five Rings, MLB (Major League Baseball), WCW Nitro, and Star Trek.

Usually beginning CCG players buy a starter set and add booster packs as they learn the game. The idea is to put together different combinations of decks that are hard to beat. CCGs challenge players to use their imagination and analytical skills.

> **Collecting Comment**
> Magic: The Gathering, originally called Mana Flash, was the first collectible card game. It was released in 1993 and received the "game of the year" award from Capital Distributors. Ten million cards were printed and expected to take six months to sell. They sold out in six weeks. Since then, nearly three billion cards have been produced and sold.

Role-playing Games

Dungeons & Dragons, the first role-playing game, came on the market in 1973. It started with three friends who liked to re-create historical battles using miniatures. This evolved into playing single characters set in a fantasy world. Game manufacturers refused to publish Dungeons & Dragons because there was no way to "win." The three gamers formed their own company called Tactical Studies Rules (TSR) and marketed it themselves. Dungeons & Dragons has grown into a fantasy world filled with wizards, heroes, monsters, and magic users even greater than its creators could have ever imagined.

Role-playing games (RPGs) like Dungeons & Dragons, Deadlands, Star Wars, and Shadowrun require

the same skills as CCGs plus lots of cooperation with your teammates. All you need is a rule book, miniatures, and dice. As players become involved they buy additional books. Sometimes they add props to create a visual kingdom with forts, buildings, walls, and a battle mat to plot campaigns.

If you're a gamer or a CCG player who's interested in becoming a collector, it's easy to do because you've already started a collection. For more information about collecting, visit your local hobby shop or go to www.wizards.com

The Cool Collector says: Because role-playing and collectible card games are their own worlds, you'd probably be a player before you become a collector.

Timeless Collections

Most fads pass their peak and people fade away or rush on to the next thing. But sometimes fads stand the test of time and become timeless collections.

Baseball Cards

The baseball cards of today came onto the field in the 1880s and were used as advertisements for a sporting goods company. Collecting these trading cards and pasting them into scrapbooks was a fad. Now, more than a hundred years later, people are still collecting baseball cards. Cards have spread from baseball to every major sport and things that have nothing to do with sports.

Baseball cards have made the transition from fad to

timeless collection. For stats on baseball collecting check out: *Sports Collectors Almanac* at the library or *The Illustrated History of Baseball Cards* and other books at www.cycleback.com. The Library of Congress also has good info at www.loc.gov. Go to "Search website" and type in "baseball cards."

> **Collecting Comment**
> The first baseball cards were handmade before the Civil War by fans pasting photographs onto cardboard backing. In the 1930s, gum companies entered the game by giving away cards in packs of bubble gum.

Dolls

Even when you get too old to play with dolls, don't pack them away. Collect them. Do your mom and grandma have their old dolls in storage? Ask them to help you create a three-generation collection.

There are hundreds of different types of dolls. If you decide to become a doll collector, you have to decide what to collect. Some dolls, like American Girls, are created to be collected. Other doll collections could be foreign dolls, baby dolls, rag dolls, or fashion dolls. When you add a new doll to your collection, save the packaging. The box is a good place to store your doll when it's not in play or on display. Original packaging can also add to the future value. Collectors who are collecting for money never even take the doll out of the box. Keeping it in mint condition in the box will increase its future value.

If you buy used dolls, look for ones that are in good condition and maybe even have their original clothing. The better the condition, the more valuable the doll. For more information about doll collecting, check out www.allaboutdolls.com.

Collecting Comment

The Barbie doll was introduced in 1959 and was named after the doll maker's daughter, Barbara Handler. The first Barbie, designed to be a teenage fashion model, had a ponytail and wore a black-and-white zebra-striped bathing suit. She was an instant success and has grown up to be a dentist, a doctor, an astronaut, a paleontologist, a soccer player, a businesswoman, and even a presidential candidate.

Model Trains

Model trains are toys that can put you on the collector's track. Trains come in all shapes and sizes. Ask your dad, uncle, or grandpa for any old trains they've boxed up and stored away. Dig them out and set up a family train station. Making displays with model trains can be lots

of fun. Some collectors even set up whole mini villages or towns to go with their train sets. You can find miniature trees, houses, people, and anything else for your model train set at your local hobby shop. For more information about train collecting, check out the Trains page on www.eHobbies.com.

Comic Books

When you want to kick back, *X-Men*, *Archie*, or *Superman* make for pretty relaxing reading. The enjoyment factor is probably the main reason to collect comic books. Although some comic books do **appreciate**—sell for more than they cost—the value of this collection is more in reading the next issue and trading with your friends or other collectors.

Still, you should treat your collection gently. Read with clean hands. (Don't let cookies crumble on your comics.) And after you read a comic book, store it with a cardboard insert in a plastic sleeve. For more information check out http://comicbooks.about.com and *Collecting Comic Books: A Young Person's Guide*, by Thomas S. Owens.

Collecting Comment

The Yellow Kid, created by artist Richard Outcault and originally published in the *New York World* newspaper in 1895, was the first modern comic strip. The Kid had a gap-toothed grin, wore a yellow nightshirt, and always looked like he needed a bath. Mr. Outcault was the first to design a strip with separate panels and speech balloons.

The Cool Collector says:
Many comic book collectors read lots of different comics, but focus their collecting on one or two series.

Hot Cars

Die-cast collectibles like Hot Wheels and Matchbox are miniature models of the real thing. Every detail is accurate down to the shape of the headlights and door handles. Working from the dimensions of a new or antique car, hot cars are scaled to $1/64$ of the original car. Die-cast cars can be collected around a particular year, model or manufacturer. For more information, check out www.toynutz.com (the website of Dana Johnson, head of the Toy Car Collectors Association) or *Hot Wheels: A Collector's Guide*, by Bob Parker.

A Cool Designer

Bob Rosas, one of the original designers of Hot Wheels, says it's a good idea to decide on what kind of Hot Wheels you want to collect, say, Fords or Chevys, or trucks or emergency vehicles. If you don't pick a theme, you're likely to be overwhelmed by the number of Hot Wheels there are to collect. He likes to poke around garage sales and swap meets for old models. Unless it's something that's really hard to find, he doesn't pay much more for old ones than new ones. Having said that, he mentioned that a pink, rear-loading beach bomb sold for more than $72,000. See it on his website at www.digiweb.com/~hwsguys under Beach Bombs.

Marbles

Marbles have been "a-round" for at least 3,000 years. They've even been found in Egyptian pyramids and Native American burial grounds. But the first perfectly round marble was produced in 1905 by a marble-making machine. There are three types of marbles to collect: handmade glass, non-glass, and machine made. For more information about marble collecting and marble clubs check out www.marblecollecting.com or the books *Aggies, Immies, Shooters, and Swirls: The Magical World of Marbles,* by Marilyn Barrett, and *Marble Mania,* by Stanley Block.

Books

Since people collect around their love, **bibliophiles**, book lovers, collect books. If you don't want to compete with your public library, specialize. Your specialty could be

your favorite author or **genre**, like science fiction or mystery. An old series like Nancy Drew or the Hardy Boys would be fun to look for at garage sales and in used bookstores. Goosebumps and The Babysitters Club are two current series that are easy to find. If you are a fan of the young wizard Harry Potter, you've begun a collection that you can build book by book.

Collecting autographed books is a two-in-one collection. Check your local bookstores and newspaper for author signings. Go to the event and have your book signed. You could take your camera and ask for a photograph with the author. If you have favorite authors, write to them through their websites or publishers and find out their speaking schedules. Authors who aren't on tour will often send an autographed bookplate on request. Again, look at their website for an address or write to them in care of their publisher. Send a letter and enclose a self-addressed stamped envelope. For details on how to do this, see the autograph section in chapter two.

A Cool Collector

Thomas Jefferson, the third president of the United States, collected books. During the War of 1812, the British invaded Washington, D. C. They destroyed the Capitol, including the Library of Congress. After the war ended, to help restart the Library, Jefferson sold his personal library of more than 6,000 volumes to Congress for $23,950. Today the Library of Congress has a collection of about 20 million books plus films, maps, photographs, music, manuscripts, and graphics from all over the world in more than 450 languages.

Board Games

As a collector, you don't ever have to be bored with board games. Call them a collection and look for them at garage sales, flea markets, and hobby shops. You can specialize in games you enjoy; games based on television shows, cartoons, or movies, or games from a particular company. Decide if you are collecting for love or money because that will direct your collection. If you are looking for future value, buy new games or used games in excellent or very good condition. But if you are collecting for love, don't be as concerned with condition. Finding a rare game—one you don't have—is what's important. For more information about collecting board games, make a move to www.boardgames.about.com.

Yo-Yos

Let's talk about the ups and downs of yo-yo collecting. An "up" is it's inexpensive to start a collection. A

"down" of yo-yo collecting is that you won't find a yo-yo shop in every mall. But you can track them down in toy shops and other places, and you'll find they have fans, clubs, and collectors. So what should you look for in a yo-yo? The yo-yo should be imprinted with its name, serial number, patent number, the manufacturer, and the year it was made. Without this information, the value goes down. For more information check out The Frequently Asked Questions (FAQ) on www.yoyodave.com or Lucky Meisenheimer's *Lucky's Collectors Guide to 20th Century Yo-Yos: History & Values.*

A Cool Collector

Don't sneeze at Nam Kim's collection! But if you do, she'll offer you a tissue from one of her many decoratively covered tissue boxes. She's been collecting them since 1997 and has covers that look like farm animals, wild animals, pianos, and faces. To see her collection, go to the Unusual Museums web page: http://www.unusualmuseums.org/, check List Sites, and look for My Tissue Box Cover Collection.

The Ultimate Cool Collector

When John Darcy Noble was six, he traded a puzzle for a friend's old and intriguing china whistle. This was the beginning of his collecting life. By the time he was a teenager he was considered an expert because of his research on the history of dolls and toys. This collecting passion led to his career as the world's first curator of dolls and toys. His collection now includes 200 antique dolls, new dolls, and dollhouses from twenty countries. Mr. Noble's collection has been shown at the Mingei International Museum, San Diego, California.

CHAPTER 4
Moving Outdoors

Open your door and look outside. The beauty of a butterfly, the brilliance of a flower, and the smoothness of a rock are natural treasures. Mother Nature provides collections just waiting to happen.

The world is full of things to be picked and preserved. There are leaves, flowers, weeds, stones, minerals, bark, grasses, shells, butterflies, beetles, moths, feathers, and much, much more. It's impossible to collect everything that grows, and swims, and wiggles, and flies, so you'll have to make some choices.

Things To Think About When Collecting Plants and Insects

- ☐ Follow the rules. Know when, where, and what can be collected.
- ☐ Keep accurate records. Write down **what** was collected, **who** collected it, and **when** and **where** it was found.
- ☐ Preserve the collection for future generations.
- ☐ Display the collection. Make it available for others to see and study.

> **A wild idea!** Collect the wildflowers in your area. The Lady Bird Johnson Wildflower Center has a list of your state's wildflowers. You can get this list by contacting the center at 4801 La Crosse Avenue, Austin, TX 78739-1702. Or access the Website at www.wildflower.org. They have lots of good information about collecting and pressing wildflowers, along with guidelines on how to collect seeds.

Collecting Plants

Let's say you start a nature collection with things that aren't going to fly away—like plants. Start a **herbarium** (a dried plant collection) from your own backyard with leaves, flowers, ferns, or anything else that grows. Before you start picking, ask the grower. (If Grandpa is planning to show his prized red roses at the state fair, they're probably off-limits.) Once you leave your own backyard, it's good manners to ask for permission and actually illegal not to. For instance, you must have the ranger's consent to collect in state and national parks. Even after choosing plants, you'll have to narrow the field down even further. Let's say you think ferns are fun and you want to focus your collection on them. You may have to narrow it down even further. There are approximately 10,000 kinds in the world, 300 of which grow in the United States. But even a fanatic fern finder would be hard pressed to gather all 300 types. So think locally. How many kinds of ferns grow in your backyard? In your neighborhood? In your county?

Before you go fern finding, look in your local library or

natural history museum for a list of friendly ferns in your hometown.

Tools for Plant Collecting

- A notebook
- A pencil or pen
- A small plastic bag for each **specimen** (sample)
- A trowel (or other small shovel)
- A pair of garden scissors

Once you find your first fern, there's a special way to pick and preserve it. This method works for all **flora** (plants or plant life). When you pick small ferns, take the whole thing, roots included. For larger plants, clip a 10-inch segment for your specimen. If there is even a chance that it is a rare species, take only a very small cutting. That way the plant keeps growing. Put your specimen into a plastic bag for safekeeping.

The Cool Collector says: Take a plant that's part of a pack. A single plant could be a sole survivor. If that's the case, its seeds or spores are needed to reproduce and repopulate the area.

Record Keeping

In your notebook record the date, the location where you found the plant, its size, and its **habitat** (the place a plant grows).

Pressing Your Plant

Once you have your specimens, taking them home and preserving them becomes a pressing matter. You can buy a plant press at a hobby store or at a science or natural history museum. You can also make your own. It's easy to construct one using boards, bricks, and newspaper. Find a dry workplace where your plant press won't be moved.

Day One

- [ ] Clean the roots of the plant as much as possible because the dirt is messy and could attract bugs.
- [ ] Choose two boards that are bigger than the specimen.
- [ ] Flatten two sheets of newspaper on the bottom board.
- [ ] Arrange the plant on the newspaper the way you want it to look when it is dried. Don't overlap the fronds. When you have plants with lots of parts, make sure each part is visible.
- [ ] Fold the newspaper over the specimen.
- [ ] Put the second board on top of the newspaper and weight it with bricks or anything heavy.

The Cool Collector says: By repeating the layers of newspapers and plants you can press and dry more than one specimen at a time.

Day Two

- [ ] Check your plants.
- [ ] If the newspaper is even slightly damp, change it. Moisture can cause your plant to mold.
- [ ] Some plants will be dried by day two, others will take longer. A plant is dried when it is stiff to the touch.
- [ ] After the plant is dried, kill any pesky bugs that might be left by sealing your specimen in a plastic bag and putting it in a safe place in the freezer for three or four days.

Mounting Your Plant

You've picked, pressed, and debugged your specimen. Now it's time to preserve it, protect it, and put it on display.

Use 100% acid-free rag paper. Choose paper large and heavy enough to support your plant. Hobby shops, natural history museums, art supply stores, and stores that sell scrapbook supplies will sell what's called **archival paper**, a high quality, acid-free paper that won't ruin your specimen. Archival paper comes in various sizes but the American Standard is $11\frac{1}{2}$ by $16\frac{1}{2}$ inches.

Before you start to glue, arrange your specimen attractively on the paper. It can be trimmed to make it fit. Think about turning one leaf over to display the back side. Leave room for the label in the lower right-hand corner.

On your label use permanent ink, India ink such as Pelikan Black Number 17, or Hunt Speedball Super Black India. Write the scientific name of the plant and the information you collected in the field.

Scientific plant name: Polypodiaceae
Common name: Maidenhair Fern
Location: 75 Green Leaf Avenue, Flowertown, PA
Habitat: The shady corner next to the fence.
Collector's Name: Jordan Beatty
Date: August 5, 2001

You need glue that is a neutral-pH formulation of PVA (polyvinyl acetate). Good old Elmer's glue fits that description. Dilute the glue with water and spread a thin layer on a cookie sheet. Gently place the plant in the glue front side up so only the back is coated. If the plant is larger than the pan, do it section by section.

Remove it from the glue and blot it on newspaper. Press the specimen onto the archival paper. Use paper towels to remove excess glue.

Add the label.

Cover the mounted plant with wax paper to keep it from sticking to anything. Put a sheet of cardboard over the wax paper, weight it down, and leave it to dry. When it is dry, store it in a tightly sealed box or cabinet.

A Bright idea

The San Diego Natural History Museum has kids out pulling weeds, not from gardens but from canyons. The students are documenting the invasion of plants that aren't native to the area. They collect, document, press, preserve, and bring their weed collections to the museum for identification. What about creating a weed herbarium of your own? Start by weeding your backyard!

Insect Collecting

Nature offers a multitude of collections. Each summer the sky is filled with butterflies, moths, and other insects. They're a tad more mobile than plants and much less cooperative. So you're going to need a net.

If you decide to become a **lepidopterist** (a collector of butterflies and moths), you'll find what you need at your local hobby shop or sporting goods store.

Tools for Collecting Insects

- [ ] A net
- [ ] Cotton balls
- [ ] Nail polish remover
- [ ] A quart-sized airtight jar
- [ ] A small piece of cardboard
- [ ] A notebook
- [ ] Small paper triangles for storage

Before You Go Collecting

Before you go into the field, you have to gather your equipment. You need to prepare a jar to kill the specimen quickly and painlessly. Soak two cotton balls in nail polish remover. Put the cotton balls in the airtight jar and cover them with the piece of cardboard, because contact with the nail polish remover will damage the specimen. Take the jar with you when you go collecting.

Along with your jar you will need some paper triangles to protect the specimen. Make these by folding an 8½ by 11 inch sheet of paper into a triangle cone. When you take your specimen from the jar, put it inside the triangle for safekeeping.

> **The Cool Collector says:** Don't chase a flying insect. Its two wings are faster than your two legs. Be patient. Stand still and wait for it to land or scoop it up as it flies by.

Collecting in the Field

Butterflies fly in the heat of the day. The best place to

look for them is where they munch and lunch. Their favorite snack spots are clover fields, flower gardens, and wooded areas. Moths fly in the cool of the night and are attracted to light. Turn on the porch light and they will come.

When you capture a specimen, stun it by pinching or squeezing the thorax, the area between the head and the abdomen. Gently remove it from the net and place it in the jar for about thirty minutes. Put only one specimen in a jar at a time so they don't damage each other's wings. Record when and where you collect each insect on the paper triangle and in your notebook. When the specimen is dead, put it in a paper triangle.

Store the specimens in the freezer until you are ready to mount them. They need to be at room temperature when you start to work.

A Cool Collection

How about a museum with more than a million butterflies.... 1,032,000 to be exact? The Allyn Museum of Entomology in Sarasota, Florida, is devoted to lepidoptera (butterflies and moths) and has collected almost 95 percent of all types of butterflies in the world. Check out their website to see just a few of them www.flmnh.ufl.edu/natsci/allyn/allyn_museum.htm.

Tools for Mounting

- [ ] A spreading board
- [ ] Insect pins
- [ ] Tweezers
- [ ] Labels
- [ ] Box with lid

Mounting the Specimen

Just like plants, you want all the parts to show. Use insect pins and position your specimen on a spreading board. A **spreading board**, a soft piece of wood made of cork or balsa, is where you dry the specimen in position for mounting.

It's easy to ruin a specimen. Work carefully and never touch the wings. Protect the abdomen from breaking off by inserting an insect pin from the tail through the length of the body. Insect pins are different from straight pins. Straight pins rust and can ruin your collection.

You may need to cross two pins like an X under the abdomen to keep it from sagging. Spread the wings to show markings and color. Let the specimen dry for at least a week before putting it into a permanent case.

Without a label, your carefully collected specimen is just another dead bug. So put on your detective hat and track down your bug's scientific name. Use a field guide to insects, or your natural history museum can help you ID your suspect. (See the plant collection sample label on page 50 for the materials to use and the information to include on your insect label.)

Remove the specimen from the spreading board. Push a mounting pin through the thorax, the label, and into the box.

You can buy special boxes called Schmitt boxes for mounting your collection. They are airtight and protect the specimen from other insects and dust. Cigar boxes or any box with a lid can also be used. You need a soft surface for the pins. Cut a piece of cardboard to fit in the bottom. If you like, cover the cardboard with felt or any other solid-color material. To order a set of Schmitt boxes and other entomology supplies, contact BioQuip Products, 17803 La Salle Avenue, Gardena, CA 90248-3602, Phone: (310) 324-07931, www.bioquip.com. Or check with your science teacher to see if these supplies can be purchased locally.

There are lots of other creepy, crawly winged critters to collect. Check out *The Practical Entomologist*, by Rick Imes, for other ideas from Mother Nature.

Collecting Shells

Sun + surf + sand + shells = A great vacation. But what can you bring home besides memories? How about a shell collection from every beach you visit? Shell shops sell unusual shells, but you can collect your own for free. That would make you a **malacologist** (a shell collector).

A Cool Collection

The American Museum of Natural History in New York has a collection of more than two million mollusk specimens (slugs, snails, mussels, clams, oysters, whelks, limpets, cuttlefish) that was created over the last 100 years through the hard work of amateur collectors. Well-documented and preserved collections by amateurs can be as much help to future scientists as those created by professional malacologists, a fancy name for mollusk collectors.

When creating a shell or fossil collection, identify each specimen with a number. Write the number as small as possible in permanent ink on the back of the specimen.

Using that number, create a database in a notebook or on your computer. Record your field collecting information. Check out *Seashells of North America*, by R. Tucker Abbott, or a seashell website at www.ofseaandshore.com.

A Cool Collector

Dr. Phil Hastings, Curator of Marine Vertebrates for The Scripps Institution of Oceanography, grew up in Florida. As a kid, he roamed the beaches collecting shells. His collecting expanded to fishes, amphibians, reptiles, snails, plants, and seaweed, some of which he kept alive in a small pond in his backyard. He's now in charge of the largest and most complete collection of coastal fishes in the Pacific Ocean from Alaska to Chile. Dr. Hastings says, "Collections, even small ones, are the best way to discover, compare, and appreciate biodiversity."

A Cool Collection

Some people collect earrings, but the Scripps Institution of Oceanography collects ear stones, scientifically known as otoliths. These small bones found in the head of fishes help them hear and maintain balance. This collection of otoliths from more than 500 types of fishes helps scientists identify species found in fossil beds.

Collecting Minerals

From gemstones to paving stones, from crystals to calcite, rocks and minerals are everywhere. You can build with them, wear them, admire them, and collect them. They're another one of nature's great and gorgeous collectibles. All the same rules of collecting, cataloging, and displaying apply. For in-depth detail about becoming a rock hound, check out http://www.sdnhm.org and go to the Kids' Habitat page and the Minerals link. Another good site is www.mamasminerals.org. Or try the books *Rocks and Minerals,* by Chris Pellant and *Rocks and Minerals (National Audubon Society First Field Guides),* by Edward R. Ricciuti.

CHAPTER 5
Organizing it All

The Cool Collector says: This may be the most important chapter in the book.

Collect*ing* vs. Collec*tions*

Once you start a collection, you'll find that almost everybody collects something. People will tell you about their great-grandfather's stamp collection that might be really valuable or the Star Wars figures they used to collect. These things may be stuffed under their bed, stacked on shelves, or stashed in closets. But this isn't really a collection. It's more like the pieces of a jigsaw puzzle.

Rather than having stuff strewn about, real collectors preserve what they collect. They take the time to assemble the puzzle. As they work with their collections, they discover duplicates or missing pieces. A Star Wars collector with three Han Solos and no Darth Vaders might decide it's time to part with a Han and trade for a Darth. Part of the fun of a collection is working with it, organizing it, and thinking about what to do next.

Categorizing and labeling a collection is the way to

put the pieces together so you know what you have. Right now it's easy to remember where your first ten model airplanes came from and who gave them to you. But when your collection takes off and you have fifty airplanes, those facts can get a little foggy unless you keep records. A collection's record is its history—the *when*, *where*, and *how* it came to be

A Cool Collector

Librarian Ann Lovell keeps files on everything she has collected for her Banana Museum. Her banana dolls, movies, pillows, clocks, art, and Christmas lights are put into categories such as ceramic items, toys, books, records, and posters. She keeps receipts and adds them up at the end of the year so she knows how much she spent. Ms. Lovell used to feel that she might be a little obsessive about record keeping. But now that her collection has grown to more than 3,000 pieces of "bananabilia," she realizes that her banana inventory is all that keeps her from slipping up. Go to the Unusual Museums web page, http://www.unusualmuseums.org/, check List Sites, and look for The Banana Museum.

Organizing Your Collection

Collections grow. Before yours gets out of control, organize it.

First create a space for working on your collection. That could be a board that you slide under the bed and pull out when you're ready to work. It could be a large basket or a box with all of your supplies. If you're sharing a work space with others, be considerate. Don't let your collection take over.

In your work space, spread out your collection (even if that means making your bed) and look for **categories**. A category is a group of similar things in your collection. Categories are the first step in organizing what you have.

Theme collection categories could be groups of similar things, like books, stuffed toys, and paper products. Other collections could be grouped by color, size, manufacturer, or the date you got it.

Documenting Your Collection

Now you are ready to make a record of everything you already have in each category. Can you remember when and where you got it? Whether it was a gift or if you bought it?

Do you know the manufacturer? The make? And how much it cost? The "when," the "where," and the "how much" are the basics of record keeping. Receipts have this information, so keep them. The more you know about an item the better. Sometimes this information makes an item more valuable. Even if it doesn't, it makes the history of the collection more interesting when you show and talk about it.

Labels

Each item needs a label. Labels can be tricky. Don't let them damage what you are identifying. With bugs and butterflies, the label is in the display box. For plants, it is printed on the archival paper. You can actually write on shells if you do it in neat, tiny letters where it doesn't show. Soft collectibles can have small string labels carefully pinned or tied to the manufacturers label. Ceramic figures can have labels on the base. Choose labels that can be peeled off easily without harming the item. Collectible cards, action figures, comics, and many other collectibles don't have a good place to put a label. Make a detailed description in your records so that each item can be identified easily.

> **The Cool Collector says:** There's a product designed to take off those pesky price stickers on your collectibles. It's called Goo Gone and it costs about $4 for eight ounces. (But be sure to follow the directions as Goo Gone can damage some work surfaces.)

Record Keeping

Let's say you're collecting elongated coins. Those are the machine-mashed pennies, nickels, dimes, and quarters stamped with the name and image of the place where you purchased it. You find them at tourist attractions, national monuments, fairs, and theme parks.

STEP 1: Divide your collection into categories. Categories for the elongated coin collection could be tourist attractions, national monuments, fairs, and theme parks.

STEP 2: Begin your record keeping in a notebook, on 3 by 5-inch cards or on a file in your computer.

Perhaps you bought your sixth coin at Ellis Island National Monument in New York. It's a penny you put into the machine and it came out stamped with the Statue of Liberty.

Your record book would look like this:

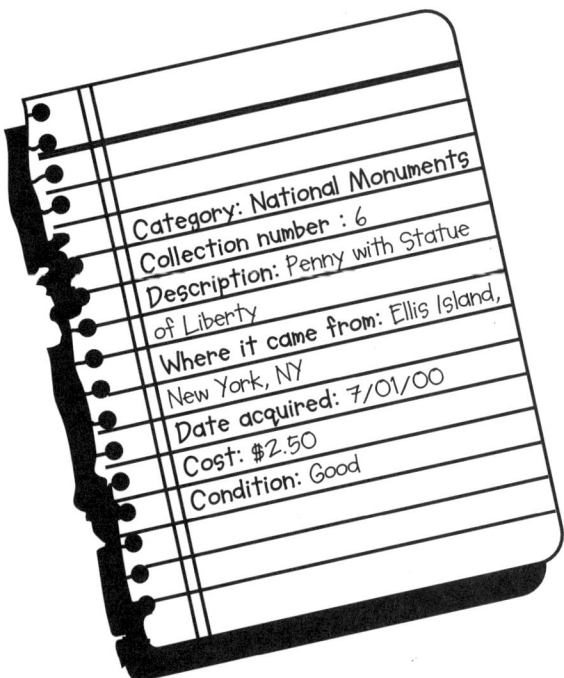

Category: National Monuments
Collection number: 6
Description: Penny with Statue of Liberty
Where it came from: Ellis Island, New York, NY
Date acquired: 7/01/00
Cost: $2.50
Condition: Good

STEP 3: Label the penny with a tiny sticky dot marked with the number 6. The number 6 links the coin to its record.

STEP 4: Store or display your collection. Keep reading for ideas on how to do that.

A Cool Collection

If you begin collecting elongated coins, you'll be amazed at all the places you'll find them. Collecting elongated coins is inexpensive. Start with the machines close to home and find them when you travel. The Penny Page, www.pennypage.com, will lead you to hundreds of locations and tell you about the club called The Elongated Collector.

The Cool Collector says: Weed, trade, and sell. If you discover more of one thing than you need, weed it out. These extras can be used to barter, sell, or trade and help you expand your collection.

Preserving Your Collection

There's a fun line between storage and breakage. Wrapping your collectibles up and storing them away keeps them safe in a boring sort of way. It's hard to enjoy something you can't see. But breakage is sad and destroys what you have worked to collect. So how can you preserve your collection and enjoy it, too? It starts with a little common sense. Keep your collectibles out of sun, rain, and dirty hands.

Collections need cleaning occasionally, especially if you play with them.

Stuffed animals may need to be vacuumed, wiped off with a damp cloth, or even dry-cleaned. Ceramics, glass,

and plastics can be cleaned with a soft, damp cloth and a mild dishwashing soap. Be careful not to scratch them. Use a hair dryer on a cool setting to dry them off before you put them away. Use a soft, dry cloth on books, videos, dolls, and trains.

Beware! These Things Wreck What You Collect

- [ ] loss of gloss
- [ ] scratches
- [ ] wrinkles
- [ ] sun or chemical fading
- [ ] pen marks or writing
- [ ] erasure marks
- [ ] stains
- [ ] warping
- [ ] rubber band marks
- [ ] gum, wax, candy, or other stains from the collectible's original packaging

Shelf Life

The best preservation for many collections is good "shelf care." Teddy bears, dolls, trains, action figures, mugs, baseball caps, paperweights, ceramic animals, and plastic collectibles can all live happily ever after displayed on a well-dusted, dry, shady shelf in your room. So can videos and books and some nature collections like shells, rocks, and minerals. Be sure that any ID labels are firmly attached to your collectibles before you put them on the shelf.

For a beginning collection, a cabinet with glass doors is nice but not necessary. As you get more involved, you'll discover clubs and websites with more details on how to care for your specific collection.

Paper Life

Your collectibles made of paper spend most of their life in storage, so make sure they're happy there. What makes paper happy is low light, low humidity, and usually lying flat. Bumper stickers, trail maps, brochures, personal history collections, bookmarks, and ticket stubs can be kept in folders, placed in a portfolio, pasted into a scrapbook, or stored in a box. All of these storage options are paper, too, and should be of archival quality. Archival quality means acid-free materials that won't yellow and crumble your collection.

Some paper collections are happiest in homes designed just for them. Autographs have their books; theater programs, postcards, and comic books have their Mylar sleeves; and stickers and decals have their own scrapbooks. Collectible cards can be kept in card boxes, plastic album pages, or clear holders for each card called "top loaders" and "penny sleeves." Don't pick up your cards by the corners. A creased corner lowers the value. Hold a card by the front and back. To keep your

collections in mint condition avoid cheap plastics the same way you avoid high-acid papers.

If you want to keep your posters in mint condition, keep them rolled and stored in tubes. You can find poster frames at hobby and frame shops for ones that you want to display.

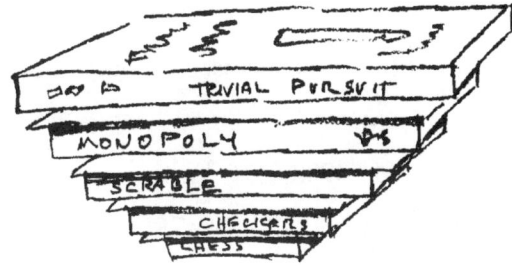

A Bright idea

To keep board game boxes in the best condition, store them vertically. Put the game pieces in plastic bags so they don't get lost. If you have limited space and have to put the games on top of one another, stack them smallest to largest like a reverse pyramid. Vertical or stacked, put a piece of acid-free paper between the boxes to protect the lids.

Storing Your Collection

Once you've sorted, recorded, and preserved your collection, you'll need a good storage system. There are hundreds of companies that create storage containers designed for every conceivable kind of collection, but you can also create your own.

So why spend money on storage that you could spend on expanding your collection? Because you are storing and preserving your collection for tomorrow. Look

for the simplest and most inexpensive way to do this, but also remember that it is worth the price to have good materials to keep your collections safe.

Boxes that slide under your bed or stack in your closet keep everything in order. Check hobby shops, game shops, container or office supply stores, and catalogs for stackable boxes. Remember the magic words "acid-free paper" and "high-quality plastic." One source for storage boxes is The Exposures Company, 1 Memory Lane, P.O. Box 3651, Oshkosh, WI 54903-3615. Write or phone for a catalog. The number is 1-800-222-4947.

When you are putting your breakables into storage, wrap them in tissue paper before you box them. Plastic collectibles don't need quite as much protection and can be slipped into plastic sandwich bags.

Humidity, the amount of moisture in the air, can be a problem in storing your collection. Have you ever pulled a shoe out of the back of a closet and found it yucky with mildew? That comes from too much humidity. If your storage area has high humidity, go to the hardware store with your parent and buy a **desiccant**, a product that absorbs moisture.

A Bright Idea

Display your marbles or beads in a big glass jar or vase. Or use muffin tins to sort and display them. A cover on top keeps out the dust.

Collecting Comment

Some collections don't have to be displayed. They can be boxed and brought out for special viewing. Your personal collection can be just that—personal. The things that you collect around yourself, such as baby clothes, old toys, and awards and diplomas, can be brought out for private viewings and special occasions.

Displaying Your Collection

Decide what you want to show off and what you want to store. Like a museum, you can rotate your collection. Put away one collection and take out another. One display idea is to rotate your collection by the seasons. Maybe you want to display shells in the summer, butterflies in the spring, and sports in the fall and winter.

Decide how you want to display each collection. Shelves aren't just for stuffed animals or ceramics, they work for itty-bitty collections, too. Things like political buttons, collectible pins, thimbles, pens, pencils, letter openers, key chains, PEZ dispensers, finger puppets, elongated coins, and miniature license plates can be stored and displayed on a shelf or in a bookcase.

But remember, flat surfaces aren't the only way to show off your collection. Think of hanging it on a wall or suspending it from the ceiling. Portable display cases are good if you want to take your collection on the road to school, fairs, or clubs. Check out the Indian River Display Case Company at http://www.indianriverdisplay.com/ or call for a catalog at 1-800-444-1280.

Shadow boxes, glass-covered cases that can be hung on the wall or set on a table, are good for both displaying and storing your small collectibles.

Look through catalogs and research your collection on the Web to explore exotic exhibiting examples. Magazines dedicated to your collection will also have interesting ideas.

The best resource is your imagination. Think about connections. For instance, if you have pins from the Olympics, you could fasten them to an Olympic T-shirt.

Baseball pins can be displayed on a baseball hat. Ballpoint pens from your travels could be clipped to a map of the United States. String a clothesline across one wall of your room and hang your natural plant collection, hats, or key chains.

Check out fabric shops and sporting goods stores for cool things that can be converted into display cases. Buy some chain in a hardware store and use the links for hanging things.

A Bright Idea

Make a quilt from your collected T-shirts. If you don't know how to quilt, look for instructions by Glenda Boston at http://www.tcnet.net/~stevens/, or to have someone else make it for you, contact Tee-Quilts at www.tee-quilts.com. Owner Sandy Kurker will take twelve to twenty-five of your T-shirts and sew them into a quilt. Check her website for the cost.

Catalogs are another source of ideas for display racks, boxes, shelves, and organizers. Some have hat racks for your baseball caps and even wooden shelves in the shape of your collectible. They also have plastic organizers with multiple pockets that can hang on your closet door and show off your stuffed animals, dolls, Beanie Babies, and jewelry. One source is Lillian Vernon. Phone for

a catalog at 1-800-545-5426, or access the Website at www.lillianvernon.com, or try Ikea at www.IKEA-usa.com.

A Bright idea

The sky is the limit for kite collectors. There are dragon kites, fighting kites, box kites, delta kites, diamond kites, and stunt kites that you can steer. Start out small with a plastic kite for under $2 and work your way up to a ripstop nylon kite for less than $15. A special birthday gift could be a 35-foot dragon kite for $45. A kite is not a kite unless it's flying, so this collection can best be displayed on a windy day. When they're not in the air, hang your kites from the ceiling of your room.

Setting the Scene

Model train collectors don't just display their trains. They build railroad stations, towns, and countryside. This kind of world can be created in scenes and dioramas for other types of collections. Each shelf in your room could have its own scene with its own story. Putting objects into a scene brings a display to life. Action figures and fast food giveaways come from books and movies whose magic you can re-create. Set the scene with props scaled to size. Use dollhouse accessories or build your own out of

Legos. Shoe boxes and check boxes can add height to your scene. Cover them with felt, shelf paper, or wallpaper. Build roads using tar paper or sandpaper, make grass from artificial turf or green carpet. Add backgrounds from calendar pages, postcards, or your own artwork.

A Bright idea

A pressed plant can be taken out of storage for a special display. You can put it in a frame without glass and hang it in your room or set it on an easel.

Self-contained Collections

Some collections such as stamps, coins, and collectible cards are so popular that they have ready-made storage and display cases. Your whole collection can be contained in one case. Hobby shops carry these types of

cases in all shapes and sizes and in every price range. Nature collections of bugs and butterflies are also self-contained collections, displayed in their mounting boxes.

When collections are contained in display cases, it makes them easy to show off. They can be taken to Scout meetings and put on display at the library. Your collections can be arranged for home viewing on coffee tables and in bookcases. Be creative and look for places to show off your collection.

A Bright Idea

Some collectors debate whether or not to keep a card in mint condition or have it signed. Others argue the value of boxed versus unboxed toys. One way to solve this problem is to buy two. One is kept unsigned and unopened and the other is open and on display.

Cool Collectors

Alexander and Susan Girard fell in love with folk art and started collecting it. They had no idea how large their collection would become. When they donated it to The Museum of International Folk Art in New Mexico, the museum had to add a wing to house the more than 100,000 toys, dolls, costumes, masks, and other folk art.

The notion that something you collect could end up in a museum may sound a little far-fetched. But when you are wondering if documenting, preserving, and storing your collection is important, think about 100,000 unorganized toys.

CHAPTER 6
Clubs, Conventions, and a Few Things More

Don't be a lone collector. There are people out there who love what you love and collect what you collect. How do you find them? Start locally. Join a club. If your collectible comes from a hobby shop or store, ask the manager about a club for kids. The hobby shop might even run one or organize collector shows.

Does your school have a club? If it doesn't, ask a favorite teacher how to start one. One way to gather members is to put an advertisement in the school paper or on the school website.

How to Start a Collecting Club

☐ Decide the purpose of your club. Some people form clubs to show their collections, exchange information, buy, sell, and trade. Others organize to go to conventions and shows together.

☐ Make flyers saying that you are starting a kids' collecting club. Post them at school and in hobby shops and toy stores that sell your collectible.

☐ Choose a time and meeting place. Meeting once a month is a good way to begin. A library or church might let you use a meeting room. Pizza parlors and ice cream shops don't mind you hanging out as long as you order something to eat.

☐ At the first meeting have everybody sign in and give his or her e-mail address. That way you have a list of club members and an easy way to get in touch with them.

☐ Brainstorm topics for future meetings. Let everyone choose a program topic to lead.

Clubs don't have to be local anymore. On the Web you can meet collectors from across the country or around the globe. Use one of these addresses to find a Web club: Collector Cafe at http://www.collectorcafe.com or eHobbies at www.eHobbies.com.

A great site is Kids' Collecting at http://kidscollecting.about.com. Every Saturday from 10 to 11 Eastern Standard Time, Robert Olson, the Kids Page host, has a chat room

for kid collectors. He could help your club set up a chat room.

The guidelines for chatting in a chat room come from common sense:

- ☐ Be polite.
- ☐ Don't give out personal information.
- ☐ Don't believe everything people tell you. It's easy to be anybody you want to be on the Web.
- ☐ Read the rules for safe surfing on the Web.

A Cool Collector

Ronald Dupont, Jr., of St. Petersburg, Florida, started collecting comics as a kid. He thinks it helped him choose a career. Two of his favorite comic book heroes, Superman and Spider Man, hid their secret identities by working for newspapers. Mr. Dupont grew up and became a journalist. He still reads comic books.

Shows and Conventions

Every July in San Diego, thousands of comic book collectors, creators, and dealers from around the world come to International San Diego Comi-con. In the world of comic books, this convention is as important as the Oscars are to Hollywood. Some fans even dress up as their favorite comic book characters. Everything from action figures to movies and toys are here, too. The Comic-con website is http://www.comic-con.org.

All conventions may not be as big and zany as this one. But most collectibles that have a national organization

sponsor a yearly convention or a series of conventions around the country. These are the places where you see what's new, what's hot, what's coming, what's out, what's old, and what's valuable.

Dealers who buy and sell your collectible will set up convention booths. Individual collectors will have smaller displays. Ask a parent, a friend, or a fellow collector to go with you. This is the place to discover what direction you'd like your collection to go in. Study what is available and set some long-term goals for what you want to buy. Shows and conventions are good places to find out what things are worth, too. Before you go, study a price guide. These are available at the library or you can buy one at a hobby shop or magazine stand.

If you have something you want to sell or trade, bring it with you. Trading and bartering are part of the fun.

Marked prices may have wiggle room. You can offer less than the set price and the seller may accept.

> **The Cool Collector says:** Keep a cool head at a convention or show. Don't get caught up in the glitz and the glitter and go over your budget. Before you go, decide what you can spend and take that amount with you.

> **A Bright idea**
> Volunteer to work at a local show taking tickets, passing out brochures, or running for coffee. This usually gets you in for free and gives you a chance to see the best before the crowd arrives. When the show is over and being packed up, there may be bargains available.

Web Shopping

You don't have to wait for conventions or shows to expand your collection. Buying, selling, bartering, and trading can be done on the Web. Cybershopping is a huge mall right at your fingertips. You have a chance to buy things for your collection that you'd never see in a lifetime even if you were a world traveler.

Find a website for your collection and start there. Look for a link for buying and selling. If the website has a chat room, ask about places to shop and the names of traders.

The same good sense that you use at a convention or show applies here. Know what you want and how much you can spend. Read your price guide and be prepared to barter and trade.

Rules for Safe Surfing from Safekids.com

1. I will not give out personal information such as my address, telephone number, parents' work address/telephone number, or the name and location of my school without my parents' permission.

2. I will tell my parents right away if I come across any information that makes me feel uncomfortable.

3. I will never agree to get together with someone I "meet" on-line without first checking with my parents. If my parents agree to the meeting, I will be sure that it is in a public place and bring my mother or father along.

4. I will never send a person my picture or anything else without first checking with my parents.

5. I will not respond to any messages that are mean or in any way make me feel uncomfortable. It is not my fault if I get a message like that. If I do I will tell my parents right away so they can contact the service provider.

6. I will talk with my parents so we can set up rules for going on-line. We will decide upon the time of day that I can be on-line, the length of time I can be on-line, and appropriate areas for me to visit. I will not access other areas or break these rules without their permission

7. I will not give out my Internet password to anyone (even my best friends) other than my parents.

8. I will be a good on-line citizen and not do anything that hurts other people or is against the law.

Buying on the Web

It's good to have a parent, friend, or fellow collector surf and shop with you. If, in fact, you are going to buy, you'll need your parents' permission. Until you are actually buying, never give out personal information such as name, address, or phone number or e-mail. NEVER GIVE CREDIT CARD NUMBERS without your parent present. If you and your parents haven't set up guidelines on Web shopping, check out the safe surfing information at http://www.safekids.com.

Be careful of any price that seems too good to be true. It probably is. Until you get to know a trader, ask for references or learn about them by posting a question on the website bulletin board or your collectible news group. Or do a search for the trader's name in a search engine. If you have a bad experience, post what happened on the website bulletin board or in the collectible news group.

Instead of a credit card, sometimes sellers want a check. If you send a check, get a phone number and address because if something goes wrong, the seller is hard to find with only an e-mail address or a post office box.

The seller may ask for a money order instead of a check because a money order is just like cash. Again, if something goes wrong, a check works better for you because you can stop payment on it. If what you are buying is breakable, ask the seller to insure it. Print out your e-mails so you have a record.

> **The Cool Collector says:** The **paper value** is the price of a collectible according to a price guide that deals with that collection. **Aftermarket value** is the second-hand price, the price the collectible can be resold for. The true value is in how much you enjoy your collection.

Selling on the Web

You can sell something from your collection on the web too. If you are a seller many of the rules stay the same. Know who you are selling to and get references if you don't. Some buyers have a history of not paying. Get actual addresses and phone numbers and keep records. Post a picture of what you are selling and be 100 percent honest. Have a return policy, which means you'll take it back if they don't like it. Pack what you are selling so that it won't break.

When you're a seller, a few of the rules reverse. Ask the buyer to pay shipping and insurance. This may be an area where you need to wiggle and negotiate about who pays for what. Since money orders are the same as cash, ask them to pay that way. Then you don't have to worry about bad checks.

Web Auctions

Another way to buy and sell is by auction. That's where you have to bid against other collectors for something you want. There are hundreds of different auction sites on the Web. Ebay, Yahoo, and Amazon are the best known but with a search engine you may find one that specializes in your collectible.

On-line auction sites give clear directions on how to bid and buy. Since they require a credit card, this is something you need to do with an adult. If you are a buyer, one good tip is to see what you are buying. If there's no picture posted, be cautious. Find out if the seller has a web page with pictures. Ask lots of questions about condition and make sure you can return what you buy if you aren't happy. If you are seller, you must decide the lowest price you'll accept before the bidding starts.

The Cool Collector says: The U.S. Post Office frowns on fraud. That's when someone doesn't tell the truth about what they're shipping through the mail. If the seller won't take back an item that you are unhappy with, you can file a complaint with the U.S. Postal Service.

A Cool Collection

A really cool collection would be snow domes or snow globes. These miniature scenes encased in glass or plastic can be turned upside down to create a snowstorm. They're inexpensive and easy to find. There are so many types of snow domes, such as cities, monuments, animals, and holidays, that any one of these could be a theme for your collection.

A Cool Collector

Elizabeth Spatz writes in style with her floaty pens. Over the past ten years she has collected more than 900 different pens from all over the world. These ballpoint pens, also called "tilt pens," have a transparent top with a scene inside. She suggests that you visit Idaho Center for the Book "Fabulous Floating Pens" exhibit, at http://www.idbsu.edu/hemingway/floaty/.

Taking Your Show on the Road
Showing Your Collection on the Web

Send your collection into cyberspace. Create a website for it. Photograph your display or photograph each piece separately. Think about what you want the world to know about your collection and create the text. It could come from the speech you use for clubs and shows. For instructions on how to make a web page, read *Make Your Own Web Page! A Guide for Kids* by Ted Pedersen and Francis Moss. Their web page is www.internet4kids.com. For on-line instructions about building a web page, go to www.geocities.com. This address also hosts web pages.

Showing Your Collection in Live Time

It's fun to share your collection with people outside the world of collecting. Look for opportunities. School is a good place to start. Ask your teacher if you can show your collection and talk about collecting. Offer to take it to other classes. Arrange with your principal to set up a display. Does your school have a hobby show? If not, maybe you can help start one. Public libraries will often display collections, too. Ask your librarian how to be a part of this.

When you set up a traveling display, make it interesting by using props such as posters and signs. Add photographs to show other collections like yours. Use maps to show the states and countries your collection comes from. To create interest, add stuffed animals, books, or miniature furniture. Try to make the display more than one level by adding height.

If you take your show on the road on a regular basis, this would be a good time to invest in a small display case that is easy to carry and keeps your collection safe. Let people know if you don't want your display handled by making a small sign that says <u>Please Don't Touch</u>. Write out a list of what you bring and check it when you pack up to go home.

When you travel with your collection, be prepared to tell people about it. Here are a few ideas to get you started:

- What is the most interesting thing about your collection?
- What made you collect this instead of something else?
- Are there famous people who collect what you collect?
- What other fun facts do you know?
- What is the best piece in your collection and why?

Outline your talk like a speech. Don't be dull. All the nitty-gritty details are only interesting to other collectors. Keep it short, ten or fifteen minutes, with time for people to ask questions. The more times you present this talk, the easier it will be.

Other great places to go and show are county and state fairs. Just like gardeners exhibit their prize petunias and kids show off their lop eared rabbits, collectors have a chance to display the best of their collections at a fair.

Most fairs have websites where you can get information. Contact your local fair board in the spring and ask for

a youth entry form. Or your collector's club can enter as an organization. Space is limited so choose carefully what you want to exhibit. Your fair display can be the same one you take on the road.

Ready, Set, Collect!

Whether you are starting from scratch or have found an invisible collection to expand, it's time to jump in and begin collecting. You know the basics and have lots of ideas on what you can collect. Let your interests guide you.

Remember, the difference between a collection and collecting is taking the time to categorize, organize, and display your collectibles. The easiest time to begin your record keeping is at the start of a collection.

Whether you're in it for love or money, the whole idea is to have a great time. That happens in different ways for different people. Some collectors are so enthusiastic they want everybody to share their love and excitement about what they collect. They join clubs, go to shows, travel to conventions, and buy and sell on the Web. Other collectors prefer wandering with a friend through a flea market or an antique store. They love the quiet time of arranging displays, creating dioramas, and recording their collection. Whichever group fits you, or if you're somewhere in the middle, you'll find a warm welcome in the wide world of collecting.